A Pokerwork of Poems

J S Langley

Copyright © 2016 & 2020 J S Langley

The right of J S Langley to be identified as the Author of the Work has been asserted by him in accordance Copyrights, Designs and Patents Act 1988.

First Published in Omnibus form in 2020 by

Apart from any use permitted under UK copyright law, this publication may only be reproduced, stored in a retrieval system, or transmitted, in any form, or by any means, with prior permission in writing of the publisher or, in the case of reprographic production, in accordance with the terms of licenses issued by the Copyright Licensing Agency.

All characters and events in this publication, other than those clearly in the public domain, are fictitious and any resemblance to real persons, living or dead, is purely coincidental.

Print ISBN 978-1-9996676-9-6

To my Mother and Father

Robert H. S. Langley (1923-2005)
Marie Langley(Lewins) (1932-2012)

Together through thick and thin
for over 50 years

With Love & Thanks from a grateful son.

Contents

1: Writing with Fire

Through The Mist 11
Precipitation 12
The N2 13
Stop Sign ! 14
I 15
Seeing round corners 16
Seeing Rainbows 17
Learning together 18
Give 20
Thanks 21
Don't 22
Let Go 24
Tubes 25
Missing 26
Awakening 28
Stupid Cat 30
Coming up for air 32
Hello 33
Stopped 34
Unsteady Steps 36
Talking to Bees 37
The Soup Pipeline 38
What's That Noise? 40
Still There 41
Teenagers are crazy 42
If you need help 44
Starlight 46

Cold on the Wall 47
Hunting for a Rhyme 48
Going at the Speed of Life 50
Back 52
Carried by a Wild Tide 54
Amber 58
Unprepared 60
I don't care 62
Knowing your Place 64
Walking the Dog 65
The Three Tenors 66
Sand Castles 68
Stung 70
Oak of Ages 72
Charmed 74
The Muse 78
Gone 79
Turning over corners 80
Coming Back 81
Highlands 82
Memory of Pain 84
Finding out 86
Home Movies 88
Outing 90
Old Enough 92
I'm Allowed to Whinge aren't I ? 94
Mirage 101
Home 102
If you knew 103
Painting with Words 104
Auction Room Magic 106

The Things That Matter Most 110
Cars 112
Stages 114
In my Dreams 115
S.O.S 116

2: Fanning the Flames

Off Colour 119
Dark Glasses 120
Cloud Shadow 121
Booking Times 122
Different Worlds 124
None that I know of 126
Ice and Sun 127
Natural Reds 128
Things we were not designed for 129
Inheritance 130
Running 132
Born to Disagree 134
Opposites 135
Deciphering Decisions 136
Fragile 138
Don't Leave The City ! 140
In the Final Analysis 142
What More 143
By the Lakeside 144
Unknown 148
Spider Man 149
Melting 150
On Wings 151

The Garage	152
Are we there yet	160
Sally	162
All the Right Moves	164
No Title	165
Deleting	167
It's life; but not as we know it	168
Strangers	170
Getting away	171
Magic	172
Not Cricket	173
The Tyne Millennium Bridge	174
The buzz that you get	175
Not for the first time	176
Wobbling	177
Patience	178
Flying	179
Lunch Break	180
Travelling	182
The Problem is	184
Three Wishes	185
Sorry	186
Elephant	188
All this way	189
Between There and Here	190
Advertising	192
The Look	193
What Cannot Be Erased	194
Zonal Differences	196
Playful Sleep	198
Good Intentions	199

1000 years 200
Stuck in the Groove....................................201
Something to wake up to 202
You...207
Golden Book 208
Bartering 210
What is Knowledge 212
View from Aesop's Bridge.........................214
Lotus 216

3: Growing Embers

Moving in the 4th Dimension 219
Cavernous...220
Sacred Object...222
First Meal 224
Group Tour 226
Beaumont Hamel 228
Smile 230
Nonsense 231
Final Frontier 232
World Heritage Site :.................................233
Between Enemy Lines................................234
Enemies...235
Sculpted 236
Who Knows 238
Sorry 240
Reflexology 242
Butterfly 243
Get a hat...244
The News 246

Playing 248
Give 'em 249
Short but Sweet 250
Full Moon 251
One Bus 252
Communicating 253
Tourist Invasion 254
Winter's Heroes 256
I'll teach you 262
Tigers 263
Holiday Development 264
The Flow of Knowledge 266
Power Cut 268
Harmony 270
Bananas 272
Lessons in Recycling 273
Juxtaposition 274
Limits 275
Reactions 276
Fragments 277
Grouchy 278
Trust 279
Completely up to you 280
Outside 282
Proof of Efficacy 283
Oppression 284
Vultures 286
Through your eyes 288
Battle of the Sexes 290
Kingfisher 292
Awakenings 293

Proving Memory is not Random................294
The Magician..296
Three Little Words 298
Picking over the Ruins 300
Age 302
The Photograph 304
Use of Language 305
Names Matter...306
Owl Box 308
Branching Out 310
Maps 312
En Route..314
Ghosts 316

John S Langley

1:
Writing with Fire

John S. Langley

Through The Mist

I see you through the mist, waiting
on the river side, the far bank,
I call but you do not hear
or see as I wave my arms
in welcome and impatience
to meet you before
it is my turn
to cross

John S. Langley

Precipitation

Drizzles, patters, pours,
soft, misty, soaking the skin
Showers

Torrential, driving, in buckets
soaking, cats and dogs
Dreich

Tropical, Summer, refreshing
heavy, gentle, light
Freezing

Incessant, warm, drenching
dewy, cold, scattered,
Stair rods

Smirr, sharp, short, sweet,
sudden, severe, intense
Downpour

Thunder, lightning, storm
blustery, horizontal, squall,
Chittering

Chattering, passing, trickling
So many words to illustrate
… an obsession with ……

The N2

On the roof of the world
another roof, flashing forks,
rumbling with indigestion,
And we, small below, shouting as loud as we can
into an unhearing noise,
drowned in the crashing tumult that throws
down tears of rain, weeping
cold shivers down
our necks

John S. Langley

Stop Sign !

Twilight and wind raised sand obscure the view,
along the unfamiliar dirt road
rutted by tourists in their mobile zoos
Looking for wildlife in a landscape
they are no longer part of
Bringing their city rules with them

And ahead we see dimly a stop sign
Familiar shape out of place
a long pole and circle atop
And we slow through long teaching
Obeying the rules
of the road
Expecting a junction

As we approach our sight clears

The circle has feathers and
raises it's ostrich head
from the ground as
we look away and drive on
Shielding our eyes
from the error and not
looking back

I

I am what there is
I am what is
I am what
I am
I
What
What is
what there is
-------------//
What there is I am

My uniqueness is a missing line,
in a gene code

John S. Langley

Seeing round corners

Can you see around the corner?
he asked

Of course not,
she said,

But if I could .....

Yes?

I would stay right here

Me too,
he said

And took her hand

Seeing Rainbows

White light
Split through glass
Rushes Over You Glowing Brilliant In Velvet
To where?
Has it come all this way to end here?
Surely not

One soul
Split through lifetimes
Revised Over Years, Genes Bellow In Veins
Who there?
Have we come all this way to end here?
Probably

John S. Langley

Learning together

We didn't know it was a wasp's nest,
Said your brothers who'd
sent you chasing a ball
into a hedge
And come running back
without it

We didn't know it was such a deep bog,
Said your brothers who'd
seen you wander off
and return
Wet to the waist
and without one of your wellies

We didn't know you were in such pain
Said your brothers who'd
visited after the op
together
And gave you a hug each
for free

A Pokerwork of Poems

We didn't know we'd have three sons
Three men now who'd
give us such grief
and joy
And teach us what love is
together

Give

Give me your pain
I want it
I'll take it off you

It'll be alright
I'd rather it were mine
You're very precious but if

only you could ……..

I know ……

you still wouldn't

Thanks

Thanks doesn't seem enough
to say

If it's the last thing
you say

But **you** know what I mean
to say

Without me saying anything but

Thanks

John S. Langley

Don't

Don't tell your dad any more dirty jokes,
He shares them with the day centre nurses
and guffaws at their false modesty
And every week
they ask for more

Don't tell you dad any more dirty jokes,
We've got our reputation to think of
He's bad enough as it is
without you
feeding him the lines

Don't tell you dad any more dirty jokes,
He only remembers the half of them
Laughing at his own telling
whilst forgetting
the punch line

A Pokerwork of Poems

Don't tell you dad any more dirty jokes,
He went missing the other day
and a neighbour called to say
'Do you know your husband's up on the roof'

And I said 'You play it and I'll sing along.'

Let Go

The sunset says 'let me go'
Deep red, spread like blood
across the sky,

'I have to go',

'Can't stay forever'

'Don't want to'

And the red leaks to grey
As your time slips away

I let you go
I have to let you go

Tubes

Lying on his back fed by tubes, chest heaving,
but still breathing

Plugged into machines;
Speaking to him, not knowing if he was hearing,
but breathing

'Come away now' we need to be leaving,
for grieving

Doctors debate the mathematics of survival
and quality of life

but the equation has no unique solution
hope is crossed fingers

Love is trying to transmute willpower to healing
to keep him breathing

He cannot leave now
What would we do
His work is not done
For us not for you

Keep breathing

Missing

I miss you when something good happens
I miss you when the phone rings
I miss you when there's a knock at the door
I miss you when the Sun shines
Or when the Lightning crackles
Or the rain splooshes down in buckets
Or when the snow falls in silent white

I miss you when something bad happens
I miss you when the phone doesn't ring
I miss you when there's no knock at the door
I miss you even when the Sun shines
Or when the Lightning crackles
Or the rain splooshes down in buckets
Or when the snow falls in silent white

Who do I tell about my life
Who do I laugh with,
Who do I cry with
Who annoys the hell out of me with
A love that is perfectly imperfect

A Pokerwork of Poems

Who do I ask
When asking is needed
Who do I listen to
When I've finally got time to listen

Where are you when I need you?

Here, around, and in,
and past and always
Do not fear
I hear you say

You were always a worrier

John S. Langley

Awakening

My first world is red and black
As vision switches on
And the boom-boom of a heartbeat
As I kick at the pliant dome
In warm constraint

Safe here and secure
Language-less, Word-less, Time-less

Floating
Floating ....

But when the world surges
my succouring sea splashes away
And my bereavement brings
the shock
of involuntary movement
uncomprehending
towards a white light

A Pokerwork of Poems

Bright, too bright

Dazzling
Painful

I cry

It is my first breath
And my first tears

Stupid Cat

This stupid cat
Hair everywhere, never been out,
Hides from everyone,
Runs from her own shadow

This silly cat
Lies on her back, a diva on legs
Learns to go out,
Bringing in 'presents'

This canny cat
Calls to be fed, bosses the house,
Purrs her way
Into our hearts

This clever cat
Mews a language, we understand
Sits on our laps
Waits to be groomed

This poor cat
Has a pedigree weakness, growing inside her
Takes to her treatment
Without complaint

A Pokerwork of Poems

This special cat
Gone too soon, lost in our arms
Buried at home
Under her tree

No cat
Like this cat, like our cat
Who still purrs
Into the night

John S. Langley

Coming up for air

I am drowning
unable to breathe
If I take a breath it would be lethal
to take in not air
but grief

I must hold my breath
For as long as possible
Until the world turns
and the air is clear

How long can I hold this breath?

Hello

Hello
You're here at last
Asleep and smelling of milk
What a journey you've had
Just to get to the start

Welcome
We didn't know
Who we were waiting for
But now we know
It was always you

Sleep
Don't mind me
We'll have time now
To get to know
Each other

John S. Langley

Stopped

Stopped

A car in an African desert
Pulled to one side of the road

We slow
But they wave us on

How strange

As we pass
we look
we look to where they are looking
and see a movement
a binocular distance away

We stop

They gesticulate us on
but we put glasses to our eyes
and we see

sleek spots
with feline arrogance

A Leopard!

The first we've ever seen in the wild
she grants us 30 seconds of her time
before disappearing
into the bush

and as they drive away past us
windows wound down
they say
'We did not think you would see our
Leopard'

It is not their Leopard
It is no-one's Leopard
It is we who are trespassing

But I only say,

'Thanks and have a nice day.'

Unsteady Steps

Take my hand
You said
As I pulled myself up on small fingers
Unsteadily taking first steps

Take my hand
She said
As we walked along the beach
Unsteadily taking first steps

Take our hand
We said
As we marvelled at new life
Unsteadily taking first steps

Take my hand
I said
As you lay in a hospital bed
Unsteadily taking first steps

Unsteadily taking next steps .....

Unsteadily
         taking
                  next
                           steps

Talking to Bees

B, bu, b, buzzzz
Uzzz, buzz, u, zz, zz
Bzzz, bzzz, u, bzz, zzz
Buzzzzzzzzz

Zzzzzzub, zzzzzzub

B, b, bu, buzzzz
Buzz, u, zz, uzzz, zz
Bzzz, u, bzz, bzzz, zzz
Buzzzzzzzzz

Talking to the bees
Telling my news
They can be good listeners
But need to be treated with respect
To avoid getting stung

John S. Langley

The Soup Pipeline

You're off to university
first one in our line
you can always rely for sustenance
on the soup pipeline

No one makes soup like you
It's probably the pound of butter
I'm sure I'll not go underfed
I'll learn to use the cooker

Keep warm and darn your socks
as holes would badly reflect
the place that you have travelled from
that should always have respect

I'm sure it'll be OK
but I am a wee bit tense
Everything is new and strange
I hope it'll all make sense

Please take this jar of soup from me
be sure to keep it upright
we don't want it leaking everywhere
and always remember to write

There's texts, emails and Skype these days,
I'll see what I can do
there might be times that I forget
but I'll never forget about you

The soup in the jar will separate
don't let it put you off
give it a stir and warm it through
it is my special broth

And when you're feeling lonely
instead of losing your shine
give me a call and increase the flow
through the soup pipeline

What's That Noise?

Music fills my head
base notes vibrate my bones
trebles send shivers down my spine

And you

And you

You are the source of the music
that moves me
disturbs me
composes
decomposes
my equanimity

But I wouldn't have it any other way

At least I'm never bored

Still There

If I try hard
I can still feel your touch

If I think about it
I can still hear your voice

I can still see your face

I can still taste the tea you made me

I can still smell the mint sauce on your yorkshire puds

I can still ....

I can ......

I ......

John S. Langley

Teenagers are crazy

Teenagers are crazy
they have hormones all aglow
that explode when least expected
and bubble and gurgle and blow

Teenagers need controlling
and keeping in at night
no tattoos, piercings or hair dye
don't let them look a fright

Teenagers are monsters
where did our children go
they were so bright and charming
now they're always saying no

We were never teenagers
no one was highly strung
these kids don't know what it was like
when we were very young

We had to keep a lid on it
be seen but not be heard
we didn't have all this freedom
weren't allowed to say a word

A Pokerwork of Poems

And now we are the parent
although it might be bad
when we are saying something
we hear our mum and dad

Good luck when you have children
and it is you that must advise
'cos we'll be there as grandparents
pretending it is wise

to remind you what you were like
when you were pretty gruff
and remember what we were like;
teenagers can be tough !

John S. Langley

If you need help

If you had less
we could help you more

If you had worked less hard
we could give you more
of our time

What a shame you have so much
maybe you could use it all,
then call us back

Why not give it all away,
move to a smaller house
and rent don't own

We always recommend that
you make sure you're penniless
before you start to lose
your marbles

If you want to take
you have to have nothing left
to give

It's only fair
We're only here
to help those
who cannot help themselves

John S. Langley

Starlight

Travelled long to reach the glassy plain
where it is refracted, despite the pouring rain
and simultaneously shimmers in the surface of a pool
is reflected, passes onwards like film on a spool

Its natural speed with slide-rule we arrogantly gauge
and confine it as a number upon a frozen page.
We note it has a spectral shift and bends upon its path
The curved space it follows we can calculate by math

It is an eon's history in a tiny point of light,
and falls upon a dreamer upon a moonless night

the sleeper's eyes are shuttered to this every-night event
with no appreciation that this light is heaven sent.

by optic nerve and evolved brain it forms a fleeting spark
lighting up a moment before it all goes dark

Cold on the Wall

Iron men of Rome
wrapped thickly with wool and woven cloth
Stamping their feet and
grumbling over their braziers

Conquerors of Europe
patrols rocked by the freezing icy gusts
of winds from the North
harbinger of trouble

Followers of Mithras
wiping the rain from their rusting chain mail
thinking of another home of
missed warmth and wine

A passing phase of
enforced invaders for a century or four
engineering to leave their mark
whilst battling against the cold

John S. Langley

Hunting for a Rhyme

Snooping through the forest
Life is just a game
Playing at being Robin Hood
No two days the same

Climbing up a mountain
Rushing to the top
Conquering the summit
Adventures never stop

Swimming in an ice-cold stream
Floating down a river
Grinning through the chattering
Never mind the shiver

Running through a meadow
Being chased by bees
Leaping through the undergrowth
grass up to your knees

Jumping off a pool side
Flying through the air
Belly flopping splashing
Life without a care

A Pokerwork of Poems

So many different things to try
So very little time
Better get your skates on
And hunt to find a rhyme

Your own Rhyme

To your own poem

John S. Langley

Going at the Speed of Life

Treacle slow
go the snail-paced seconds
waiting for a bus
wanting to be old enough to...
watching the clock tick, tick, tick
Hoping for something to happen
Anything to speed up the slow creeping
passage of time

Creeping past
go the unforgiving minutes
trying new things
taking fresh steps
telling new tales
Hoping that it will all happen
Soon, the sooner the better as it's
approaching your time

All too fast
go the immortal days
nothing's too much
needing to run faster
no stopping or looking back
Hoping for everything to happen
All at once, to cram in each crevice as
much as time can stand

A Pokerwork of Poems

Invisibly passed
go the fleeting years
building a career
buying a house
bringing up kids
Hoping for nothing to happen
Nothing to derail the express train
you're riding

Treacle slow, creeping past, all too fast,
invisibly passed, then at last

Slow goes the clock

when it's reaching its stop

Tick
       Tock
              Ti............

Back

Back, back, back, back
Never looking back
Always looking forward
to a future not a past

Back, back, back, back
Never going back
To the one place that I held to
that never held me back

Back, back, back, back
I am going back
For a visit not a return
a reminder of what's passed

Back, back, back, back
I am thinking back
Can you hold a place so closely
If it's changed and can't come back

Back, back, back, back
Always going back
Searching for a reason

      Searching for a reason

           Searching for the reason

That I can't get back

John S. Langley

Carried by a Wild Tide

In green dream time two brothers play and grow,
building their knee-scraped confidences
while their mother protects them both
like a knife.

Cut short is the laughter as the War comes
The drum-beats taut on the mother's brow
as her Andrew, the eldest, enlists
and hasty Colin lies away two years of life
to join the other friendly names
on the smiling recruitment roll.

Home is left bleeding for training and mess,
Green washed away through
the Drill Sergeant's taunts
as they learn to stomp to readiness.

1915 then warms them to France
and the future narrows, marks their time
to trenches and the shelling whine.

A Pokerwork of Poems

***

At home an ageing mother
stoops over their unslept beds
folding corners that have not been creased
whilst sons write home
saying they're "just fine"

Through time she tries not to read
between their lines

as in a confusion of sounds, lights and lead
they swim the high mud-sea side by side
out into the goo that slows to a pant
a headlong charge, and in the wild tide
a shell falls too close
and finds it's nourishment.

John S. Langley

***

Parted
They come home by separate roads

Colin a weeping wound that brings him back
Invalided

Andrew deafened,
a P.O.W who escapes home
by a longer way

With the tide spent for now, for now
Both try not to sink
under the weight of their new loads

A Pokerwork of Poems

*****

At the war-end ebb tide
beached flags start to flutter
heralding a future for the old home town

and in the street, the marchers
celebrate the great victory
and the crowd surges and cheers

Whilst one straight-backed unhearing marcher
with stubborn pride
reaches out into the throng

to take a hand
and slowly
that is fast for him

to walk
hand in hand as Brothers
slipping through the cheering chaos

Looking straight ahead

John S. Langley

Amber

Salt water crusted
fished from the sea
after a journey of 40 million years
an Eocene capsule

Stickily capturing
bits and pieces
in resin exuded from conifers
in forests, unharvested

Unmolested by
the toolmaker
38 million years distant in
an unfathomable future

Fossilised colour
white to black-blue
infrared micro analysed
as proof of veracity

Encased time
extinct genera
fauna and flora inclusions
a unique contribution

Polished to shine
sunlight reaching anew
interior landscapes
worn to adorn

Revealed again
shards of a frozen world
science, art and Time
inter-twined

John S. Langley

Unprepared

Nothing prepares you
for your child needing a lifesaving operation
For signing a piece of paper that hands
him over to a stranger
who is going to cut him deeply
to do him good ....
you hope

Nothing prepares you
for the five and a half hours you have to kill
for what to talk about
when there is only one thing on your minds
that you dare not talk about
because ......
you hope

Nothing prepares you
for the surgeon's demi-godly words
'I am happy with how it went'
when there are so many things to ask
but you can't say anything
except ....
thank you

and now hope can start to turn to belief

can start ....

again

John S. Langley

I don't care

The Seller's side said
it wasn't their fault
The Buyer's side said
it wasn't theirs
I don't care

The nurse said
it was the Doctor's fault
The Doctor said
she did the wrong thing
I don't care

The Judge said
the Jury made a mistake
The Jury said
they were misdirected
I don't care

The Parent said
the Child never listened
The Child said
he couldn't hear for the shouting
I don't care

The Teacher said
the Students should have got higher marks
The Students said
they couldn't understand a word he was saying
I don't care

A Pokerwork of Poems

The Lecturer said
all her Poems amounted only to doggerel
The Poet said
it was 'free verse' and to leave her dog out of it
I don't care

The Lawyer said
millions must be paid in compensation
The Defendant said
an 'Apple Pie Bed' wasn't worth that much
I don't care

After the event analysis is always
easier or tribal
Who doesn't enjoy the blame game game
I don't

If something is wrong fix it!
If it can't be fixed
learn and grieve
and don't do it again!

Care, Care, Care

John S. Langley

Knowing your Place

Arms outstretched to embrace the velvet night,
Pierced by the pin-prick past of stars,
Glowing red, blue, amber, yellow, white

Ululating chants pant from a heaving chest,
Calling for a oneness of belonging,
An equal partnership with the whole

But the sky does not hear
and with the petulance of a weeping child
the voice cries threats
that crack the glassen sky
to shards of jealousy,
that fall as spears, around and through,
nailing his feet to the earth;
and a return to silence

Walking the Dog

That bloody dog
I'm sure I tied him up outside
no doubt some helpful hand had set him free
to enter the bar and cause utter havoc

That blasted dog
if he needed to empty his bladder
why did he have to first go secretly behind the bar
and cock his leg over a crate of bottled beers

That barmy dog
having done the deed to cries and shouts
why did he have to wander nonchalant and oblivious
to my feet and look up at me wagging his tail

That expensive dog
No need to ask whose dog it was that couldn't
read the 'No Dogs Allowed' sign hung prominently
No need to ask who would pick up the tab

for the damage
and walk the dog home fuming as it gambolled
alongside, big eyes glistening with contentment
and pride in bringing me home so promptly

John S. Langley

The Three Tenors

I bought him a cassette
The Three Tenors
Pavarotti, Carreras, Domingo
letting rip on a warm Italian night,
under the stars in 1990
in the ancient Roman baths
to celebrate
World Cup Football

Conducted by Mehta
a No.1 Album
70 weeks in the UK charts
surprise global success story
rejuvenating the classics
Nessun Dorma, Puccini
Granada, Lara
Solos, medleys and encores

It was only a tape
played to destruction
until Maria was only a mumble
O Sole Mio jammed
O Paradis incomprehensible
played until the tape
was nearly rubbed clean,
frayed, twisted and rewound

with a pencil, several times
needing replacement

Why didn't he buy another?

There was no other
that could replace that
tape, that he played
sitting alone in the car
engrossed, eyes closed, dreaming

I bought him that tape

In a Sale

Sand Castles

Footsteps in the fresh receding wetness
indents filling with seawater
small buckets, small hands, and spade
Digging
deep
Building
a uniqueness, impregnable
with a moat
In hours
with sun on their backs
with sun cream on their backs

Shouting at the sea for coming in
creeping towards the defences
it advances against the wishes of Canute
Tidal
breaching
falling
a uniqueness, vulnerable
washing away
in minutes
with the lowering of the sun
with the lowering of their sun

A Pokerwork of Poems

The flat wet plain exposed again
awaits new architects
with small spade, bucket, hands
Scooping
shallow
moulding
a new temporary uniqueness
to be washed away
soon enough
in the cycle of the tides
in the cycle of our tides

John S. Langley

Stung

Only 3 and Autumn leaves
red and brown, yellow and orange
litter the pavement
Crinkly and crisp

The small hand reaches to touch
a pretty leaf but not knowing
what hides beneath
Yellow, black striped

On its last legs but not gone enough
to miss the opportunity
to sting acid deep
little plump fingers

that wrap like tentacles and
recoil in pained surprise
to cry and show
in palm of hand

the culprit to be dispatched
The agony so intense
I can still feel it
down the years

A lesson that needed only one telling
and sixty years later
I still look beneath
before I pick anything up

John S. Langley

Oak of Ages

An acorn shed into the welcome warmth of earth
as a Danish King tries to hold back the sea
grows through the Conquerors arrival, the
building boom of castle keeps and mottes

Escapes the Armada's defense call
and unknowingly inhabits freshly united ground
that is threatened by an ambitious Frenchman
who instead turns to unforgiving snows

Victoria reigns and an Empire grows less sturdy
than its girth of gnarled and knotted trunk
and is tempered, tested, cracked and broken
after millions die twice over and an atom is split

Now I stand before you, grown past maturity
unhuggably large in girth and look at this year's
fresh green growth of undulated leaf and
underfoot step gingerly around your fruits and shells

that feed the squirrels and give promise of
a new generation rooted in the neighbourhood
away from your now empty heart full of the buzzing
of bees, the scuttling of transitory mammals and

birds that linger in your arms and chatter over the
nesting sites of a Summer's needing as if lives
depended on it - and they do
and did you blink and miss me

I did not miss you

John S. Langley

Charmed

I was sent out to get the fish suppers
5 papers; 2 Haddock, 3 Cod
I thought I was going alone but
by the time I'd picked up the car keys
he was already at the door
with his coat on
and a smile from ear to ear

Entering the shop we joined the queue
'Hello Mr Langley,' the lady called
over the heads of everyone
in her white grease streaked pinny
'Shall I put you a Haddock in?'
'Ooooh, yes please' says he
'Could you make that two' I add politely

to be answered by an icy stare
'This is my son' says my rescuer
'Oh, OK then' and a smile
and by the time we make it to
the stainless steel mirror polished counter
the fish is ready
'I'll put you in some batter bits'

A Pokerwork of Poems

And she leans forward to confide
'There's also a few extra chips in there
and a little tub of curry sauce.'
I paid and carried the bag that was
heavier than expected, handles pincer tight biting
into my hands whilst I bore it manfully
I did not complain, suffered in silence

'See you soon' , 'Oh aye you will'
'Thanks very much' I called over my shoulder
but received no answer, I just had to accept
that I had been in the presence of greatness
An example of special treatment
but at least I knew, that if I played my cards right
I'd get to share the extra chips

John S. Langley

***

We got back to vinegar, ketchup and warm plates
waiting with the bread and butter and
placed the plastic carrying bag on the table
taut with its load, newspaper warmth exuding
that unmistakable smell of welcome
'How did it go' , 'Oh just fine
we had no trouble at all'

The portions are opened
comments are made
'They serve a good portion of chips'
'Yes they do'
'Bob here's your seat. I've buttered your bread'
'John there's some for you over there
if you want it'

As I tucked into the dribbling beauty
of a chip butty
enjoyed the crisp batter of the whale sized
white fleshed, haddock
the crunch of the batter bits
I could only ruminate

A Pokerwork of Poems

Charm

You're either born with it ...

...or you're not

John S. Langley

The Muse

No sooner has she arrived
than she is tapping
her fingers

on the corner of the coffee table
impatient to be
on her way

Pausing only to clap her hands
once, twice, thrice
in my ears

So that an inner voice is awakened
to whisper words
to my pen

And I can write without control of
the real content or
the meaning

Too soon she makes a small gesture
and gets up to go
too soon

And leaves me to finish off as
best I can
alone

Gone

The clock stopped
And did not go again

That's how we knew
It was real and unchangeable

Like a mechanism
That cannot be restored

Run out of its time
Been well used and loved

We looked at what was left
And tried not to cry

John S. Langley

Turning over corners

Turning over corners
to remember where you're up to
as a quick way to get back
to some special place

Turning over corners
as a marker of something important
that you'll know how to find
if you were to forget

Turning over corners
as a wanton act of vandalism
have you no respect for the book
it cost so much to buy

Turning other's corners
as a mark that you were here
how can they forget you as long as
the corners are turned

Coming Back

As I was coming back from Poole
I was sure that all was cool

As I was coming back from Coombe
I heard a loud explosive boom

As I was coming back from Slough
I wasn't as sure as I am now

As I was coming back from Bow
I wasn't thinking where to go

As I was coming back from Blean
I was still going and still keen

As I was coming back from Dover
I was feeling like a rover

As I was coming back from Lens
I began to realise I was badly lost

John S. Langley

Highlands

An empty house
The car is full of the last removals
and the key turns in the lock for one last time

On the threshold
the years reel and replay
Christmases, snow cold, turkey and wrapping paper

Through the windows
the sound of laughter and play
laying carpets, fixing the damp, repairing the roof

Outside, the street
neighbours who enriched our lives
parking a problem, normal ups and downs

Fantastic views
pit ponies graze the back fields
size of a big dog, sheep sheared and swallows swoop

In reach of
parents to whom visits were precious
but as 5 we needed a bolt hole and found it here

Time's wheel
has now turned past these moments
children have left the nest and parents no longer held

Goodbye, Good Luck
the keys are impatient to be passed over
someone else's turn to redecorate, fix the guttering

So to be not a house
but a home
again

And for us memories
family-spread
unforgettable

So it just remains to say
Thank You
Thanks
Tacka
Ta

John S. Langley

Memory of Pain

The pain was intense when I broke my leg
in two places
And bone pushed out against the skin
like an alien birth
Each driven bump on the road to the hospital
slicing through me like a knife
scorching me to the soul with a devil's fire that
consumed my whole world

I know this to be true as I have a memory of it
but not of the pain
The body wracking intensity of the agony
has dissolved away
the pain is verbalised, intellectualised, unreal
not felt anew, a paper thing
and I struggle to imagine anything that could have
filled my reality so completely

The pain was intense at the funeral parlour looking
into the open coffin
at inanimate skin that bone pushed against
like an alien thing
each remembered nook and cranny, smile and groan
slicing through me like a knife
wounding me to the soul with a dull ache that
consumed me utterly

A Pokerwork of Poems

I know this to be true as I have a memory of it
and feel the pain
in Remembrance seemingly undulled in intensity
and see and taste and touch
the pain as real, visceral, and raw
felt anew, a solid thing
and I struggle to imagine anything that could ever
prevent my remembering

John S. Langley

Finding out

Emails are set to beep their arrival
on my phone
Short of time I left an absent bid
on an auction site

Forgetting what I had done I sat idling when
the phone beeps
and looking at my watch I realise
what it might be

So now the outcome is known and fixed
whether I had won or not
was an electronic fact set in stone
News waiting for me

Had I won?
Had I lost?
How many bids had there been?
What was the winning bid?
Had I left a bid too high?
or too low?
Would I be pleased if I'd won?
Would I be relieved if I'd lost?
and saved the money
How long could I wait before I needed
to find out

A Pokerwork of Poems

I looked across at the waiting, winking screen
This was time enough
I reached across, accessed the emails
Scrolled down

And found out I'd ....

John S. Langley

Home Movies

Click
Whirr
Hunnnnnnn
The video tape turns
and the screen flickers
and settles
and sounds and pictures come to electronic life

Home
movies
resurrection
The faces animated
with voices familiar and clear
in accents
and here again, returned in recording to be again

There
on screen
talking on camera
making bad jokes we've
heard before but now laugh
because
they're not funny, but well remembered

A Pokerwork of Poems

Here
once more
returned to say
Hello, out of the mists
on camera that was just a bit
of fun
but now are all that is left of those snapshot days

Whirr
Click
Swoooosh
The old tape re-boxed
the screen flickers empty
and settles
to other sounds and pictures designed to entertain

John S. Langley

Outing

Walking past a butcher's shop
the three of us and our Dad

Accosted by smells of roasting pork
peas pudding, crackling and stuffing

Dad wasn't rich but he wasn't mean
and we looked at him imploringly

He gave in easily ; we went inside to buy
Don't tell your Mam or I'll get shot

Promises made we peer and slaver
as the sandwiches are prepared

Layer on layer of goodness overflows
and drips fattily down the sides

But wait, what's this, there's been a mistake
there's four of us and they're making only two

In a fever of vexation I point this out to Dad
who slaps his head in forgetfulness

A Pokerwork of Poems

And speaking over the counter says
'I'm sorry I forgot something important .....

I forgot to say,
      .... can you cut them in half please' !

And they did

And I can still taste them

They tasted good

Walking down the street secretly eating

Half a sandwich with

My two brothers

And our Dad

John S. Langley

Old Enough

My Grandad used to sing to me
About a Preacher and a Bear
And if I had a lucifer to light my fag
But I didn't know what he meant
as I sat on his knee
singing along anyway
to the consternation of my Gran-ma

My uncle used to tell me of the war
Of when he was blown up and
captured and escaped and found
his way back home somehow
And his sister used to say
stop filling his head
with that stuff - it's not important

My Dad told me when he got older
a few things about Africa and
Sicily and Italy in 1943
And said even though you like
playing with pistols and guns
shooting at ghosts
stay away from the real thing - it's not fun

A Pokerwork of Poems

And I'm old enough to have stories now
Of travels and experiences and
lots of interesting people I've met
that I relive in the telling
even though it was in times of peace
No bullets flying
Good to pass them on - before they evaporate

And I'll sing to the grandkids
And tell them secret stories
That they won't understand
Even when they're old enough
That'll be good !
That'll do me

John S. Langley

I'm Allowed to Whinge aren't I ?

Instead of discipline at school
Instead of trusting the police to do their jobs
on our behalf
Instead of daring to protect ourselves
or our country
in case we hurt people's feelings
in a dangerous world

Instead of fearlessly speaking out
Instead of saying 'Thanks' to the NHS
for all they do
Instead of having the confidence
to get things done
and manufacture our own stuff
whilst developing our skills

Let's mosey down the PC Plughole
All go down the PC Plughole
So much easier
and so much fun
to complain
than take responsibility

Let's all stand back and
let it happen
There'll be so much more
to complain about

John S. Langley

*

Let's put every infrastructure decision
to a committee of 10's
and listen to every minority
over and over again

Every point of view
viewed with equal weight
vacillate and prognosticate
decision taking can wait

Allow Countless appeals to keep
the lawyers fed

stay paralysed by PC
whilst others pass us by
smiling and waving
Waving us bye-bye

*

Thank goodness we're so civilised
so inclusive and so fair
A model to all others of
how to care

Smiling in contentment in
our aged public buildings
not noticing that they're crumbling
round our ears

Knowing that if we put a step wrong
Our media will set us straight

Or bring us down

John S. Langley

*

And on the News please tell us
of all those things
that have gone wrong
or can go wrong

Don't major on the areas that
we should improve
we can improve
we have improved

Please leave us feeling pretty glum
and fearing for the future
After all its what we deserve

Isn't it?

A Pokerwork of Poems

*

The media is an industry
one of our most successful sectors
Manufacturing stories
Manufacturing News

Filling lots of pages
Filling hours of time

Delivered to the customer
Directly to their homes
We don't even have to get up
to be spoon fed

You are what you eat
Believe what you hear

John S. Langley

*

Here we go down the PC Plughole
PC Plughole
PC Plughole
Here we go down the PC Plughole
All day long

How could the bath not be filling
when the Plughole's in full flow

Mirage

The silvered glass lies an image
Not recognised
Reversed
But not flattering

A crackled tone accents a message
Left in a voice
Recorded
Known but not known

Sepia stained photos shimmering
Album confinement
Unconserved
Capturing gone times

In these things I don't see me
I don't hear me
Who is this
Who was this person

John S. Langley

Home

Home is a peopled place you create
a corner of space and time
with select emotions and experiences
that jumble and rub along together

Home is no place like utopia rather
it is where you choose it to be
that gives you the anchor you need
for your uniquely personal journey

It is the centre of the circle around which
you radiate and revolve
a place that may not really exist
except in your own head

It is full of memories, good and bad
that are stuck indelibly in your mind
It is where you always want to get back to
as long as you never do

If you knew

If you knew you would die
Tomorrow
What would you do
Today

If you were sure this was the
Last time
What would you want to
Say

If you knew you would die
Tomorrow
What would you want to
Say

If you were sure this was the
Last time
What would you do
....

John S. Langley

Painting with Words

Your gaze embraces a red sky horizontally
streaked with clouds,
white-grey above their brazen underbelly
The scene spreads, wider than your open arms
can reach
And below is a rippled sea, bronzed by reflection
See, look, take in the view

There is a light, cooling breeze coming
off the water
It blows in your face, drifts through your hair
makes your eyes water so that you reach up
to wipe away
the fake tears, whilst moisture coagulates
and trickles cold down your neck

Your open mouth takes in a deep breath
and catches
the salt taste of the air that activates your tongue
before hitting the back of your mouth as
you gulp the air
freshness into your lungs, the sweetness of it
takes your senses by surprise

A Pokerwork of Poems

The water washes shushing on the
sloping shore
a whoosh, whoosh melody that smooths the sand
whilst the gulls cry the day to its end and
the breeze
echoes in your ears like seashells, the whole
orchestra making a melodious melange

Your nasal passages explore
the parts-in-a-million molecules
of odour that tickle and tantalise
the receptor sites
and fire sensations of crispness and briny essence
that flavour your whole world and wrap you
into the place
anchoring it as
real
and present
and now

Painted by words no longer

John S. Langley

Auction Room Magic

Saw it, scrutinised it
looking for scratches
feeling for cracks
and other faults

Searched the internet
for prices and value
to set a sensible limit
A 100 should do it

Come the day
the room is full,
the internet is working
A 100 should still do

What are these people
doing here today
Have they nowhere
else to go

An hour passes and
lots are bought and sold
Coal scuttles, bowler hats,
reproduction canon

Didn't bid, held back,
keeping powder dry
Now only 5 lots away and
palms begin to sweat

Can feel a heart rate
increase, pupils
dilating while straining
to keep on looking cool

This is it

Someone start me at 200?
No
100?
No
It's surely worth 50
A bid
50, Thank you

And so we go
by 5's and 10's
It does not slow
and breaches 100

John S. Langley

I close my eyes
raise a hand and
leave it there
and stop thinking

160, 160
Is that it
Are we all done

160, 160

Bang, SOLD

I got it, I won
Was it more important
to win than
stick to 100

Yahoo, Eureka,
now all I need to do
is to think about how
best to utilise it

A Pokerwork of Poems

What do you do

with a life size
fibre-glass

Gorilla?

John S. Langley

The Things That Matter Most

He didn't talk too much about the war
or his part in it
Most of his experiences could not to be spoken of
to the uninitiated
but he did tell of a time in Italy
when he had to take a message quickly
and borrowed a motorbike
from his mate Jack

In the dark he drove over broken roads
a scarred landscape
With only a slit light to show the shattered way
He succeeded in
his mission and with a lighter heart
turned and rode a bit less carefully
Hoping there would still be food
when he got back

He didn't know that one of the bridges had just
been blown and a black hole gaped
into which he flew like a stone and dropped
into a grimy hard
cold wetness that drew blood and covered
him in a thick slick mud of putrid stench
as he gasped up at the stars
lying flat on his back

A Pokerwork of Poems

No bones broken but scraped and bruised
he emerged painfully and
stumbled onto the road to make his way
trudgingly homeward
going through the story he had to tell of how
lucky he was to have got away with it
and still be whole though his head
had suffered a crack

Back came the conquering hero
bloody but unbowed
home to his mates and his comrades
dazed and muddied
but ready to receive the cheers and applause
And there was Jack his mate, first to
greet him, standing at the door
who rushes forward shouting
What the hell have you done with me bike!?

John S. Langley

Cars

Cars are just mechanical contraptions
a collection of parts of various materials
brought together, cooled and lubricated
to get us safely from A to B

Except my Car

Cars have no personality nor emotion
It is ridiculous to suppose that talking
to your car would make it run any differently
in any possible way at all

Except my Car

To invest your car with a name is a symptom of
lunacy that needs immediate medical
attention before it reaches the point of no return
and you start to talk of it as family

Except my Car

My Car on the other hand is like an extension of me,
like a handshake we fit together. George would
never let me down on purpose and responds well
to the gentlest of flattery

A Pokerwork of Poems

That's my Car

The one and only Car that understands
me properly

John S. Langley

Stages

Born as an I
Searching for we

Becoming an us
What's all the fuss

Clean out your rooms, stop all the noise,
Careful with that, they're not really toys,

What did we do
Before we had you

I need some peace to finish this week
What did you say, you're so full of cheek,

Be careful what you wish for!

In my Dreams

In my dreams you are there
young, as you were when
we first met
all those years ago

In my dreams I climb the mountain
easily, as I used to do
stones crunching
under well-worn boots

In my dreams the Sun shines
brightly, between clouds
lighting my face
bringing warmth to life

In my dreams I am in control
uniquely, switching from
scene to scene
You are in my dreams

John S. Langley

S.O.S

Indexing memories
Smells
Smiles
Sounds
Salty Fish and Chips

Playing the notes
Out
Of
Order
On a Sunday morning

Following the Rules
Simply
Squarely
Silently
Sssending out .....for help

2:

Fanning the Flames

Off Colour

I got the Blues
I got it Black today
I got the Blues
Just got to get away

Away from the messing
Back to Greener ground
Got to stop guessing
Got to get homeward bound

Past the Red burning
To calmer waters
No more of the running
To other's orders

I got the Blues
I got it right today
I got the Blues
But I let it get away

John S. Langley

Dark Glasses

If an elephant wore dark glasses
would it be in disguise

If you put a sheepskin on a dog
would it pass for a lamb

If a tiger rolled over on it's back
would it be safe to approach

If I say sorry and really mean it
would you listen to a word

If I honestly tried to stop pretending
would you think it a disguise

If I turned and ran towards you
would you think me on the lam

If I told you what was on my mind
would you meet me with reproach

Is it too late, is it too late or
might some pigs still fly

Now please take off those Sunglasses
Were you listening to me at all

Cloud Shadow

Dark patchwork fleeting
over
moving on between bright
places
Lacing meanings to dreams
images

Washing over grey shades
shadow
Transitory temperance amongst
turbulence
Presaged passing past and
gone

John S. Langley

Booking Times

The rolled pulp squeezed and
flattened
does not decide
what ink dyed language
is indelibly dripped through its fibres

It's one virgin sullied chance at
immortality
is in the minds
of strangers pushing levers
and griping at the costs of the overheads

A collected classic or one of the
leftovers
in the bargain bin
Value determined by fashion
or rarity of hieroglyphics and meaning

to some human need or pushing
forward
the boundary edge of
knowledge or culture or belief
unconscious vehicle of controversy

A Pokerwork of Poems

Held in the hand or attacked by
beetles
or defiled by unkind
moisture or Sun blanched by time
despised by unbelievers and burnt

Defenceless impersonal artful
objects
centuries leading to be
replaced by electrons maybe or
recognised irreplaceable co-conspirators

Time will tell - and we'll write books
about it

John S. Langley

Different Worlds

There was a man crossing
the road
slowly
and his gait told that
he was a man of the land and
that this was the speed that he went at

Waiting impatiently I had time
to think
slowly
that he probably did more
going consistently at one pace
than I at my sprint and pause, sprint ...

A Pokerwork of Poems

And when he finally passed over
and aside
slowly
he turned raised a hand
and waved and turned away
again as we went our separate ways

John S. Langley

None that I know of

What living thing can
exist alone
None that I know of

What world can
exist forever
None that I know of

What time can
travel backwards
None that I know of

What words said can
be unsaid
None that I know of

What memories are
infallible
None that I know of

Ice and Sun

Ice and Sun are strange bedfellows
as they creak and twist
their public embrace
Lighting Winter's embers into
cold yellow as flame

In perpetual battle North to South
giving and not giving
quarter to each other
Pulsing in time to the heartbeat
of all our heartbeats

John S. Langley

Natural Reds

A Red Mason Bee vies with the
Red Admiral to take sweetness
from a handful of Red Raspberries
late fruiting

The Red of the watching breasted
Robin vies with the Red wattle of
the male Ring-necked pheasant
ladybird red

A Red squirrel skitters through the
hazel branches ignoring Red firebugs
that ignite the Sun-setting sky
lobster red

Things we were not designed for

Flying
Sailing
Keeping Bees

Deep Diving
Space travel
Talking long distance

Writing
Shooting
Snapping Photographs

Coping
with the loss
of a loved one

John S. Langley

Inheritance

You can have this
when I'm gone
It's worth a lot
of money

This is very nice
it was gran's
over 100yrs
older now

We need to decide
who gets what
before we sell
the house

Sell, give it away
I don't want
any of it
anymore

As a memory we'll
take something
to remember
something

A Pokerwork of Poems

Take, leave, sell
divide, don't
need, want
anything

Getting it done
finally, we
have some
stuff

but honestly
we would
rather
she hadn't gone

We could do
without it
but can we
do without ......

John S. Langley

Running

Water
Noses
Feet

Sand through hourglasses
Clocks that tick
Wounds that won't heal

Into
Over
Out of

Jokes that repeat every Christmas
Down the lane with no end
After the one that got away

Along
Across
Around every corner

A Pokerwork of Poems

Away

        Away

                Away

                        Away

John S. Langley

Born to Disagree

It's mine not yours
Get your stinky paws
off it

They're white not black
You always go into attack
before thinking

You still don't understand
This isn't how I planned
it was going to be

Don't cry, I'm sorry
that life is full of worry
for the both of us

Come back to bed
We can argue some more
over breakfast

Opposites

The clarity of the Black White
Dichotomy
North, South
Positive and Negative
East, West

If there was on thing of certainty
that could be relied upon
It was the paired dipole clarity of
the fixed and stable meaning
of opposites

That was before we had three sons
and life and meaning got
clearer and more complicated
and we realised that they are
all opposites

John S. Langley

Deciphering Decisions

She loves me, she loves me not
I want to hold on
to what we got

She riles me, gets under my skin
Wants always to know
where exactly I've been

Been sort of together for a couple of years
Got to decide now
if we move up the gears

But I'll chew it over
like a dog with a bone
What is the right thing
the wrong thing
is this the one

A Pokerwork of Poems

I feel like a man at the edge
of a cliff
looking over the edge
knowing he needs
to jump off

Needing to jump
but scared I might fall

or like a fledgling
fearing
to take
its first flight

John S. Langley

Fragile

The atmosphere is changing
being pumped with CO2
It's us that's tipping the balance
and it's us that haven't a clue

what are the consequences
of our actions to ourselves
or what to do about it as we
ignore the clambering bells

The components of the air
have and are forever changing
while our planet evolves
one thing is clear:

It's not the atmosphere that's fragile

It's us

John S. Langley

Don't Leave The City !

We live rurally and we want
all urban dwellers to know
That it is really horrible out here
so close to land and dirt and stuff

Don't be fooled by the odd sunny day
the weather is mainly rain and fog,
toads and locusts and bitey things
and not a coffee house for miles

The further North you go the worse it gets;
so much space and strange accents
that you need a phrase book to get by
and even complete strangers like to chat

Stay in your cities with everything on tap
that you could possibly want or need
Where culture is refined and the world's
chefs vie for your taste buds expensively

Don't venture away from your busy streets
or consumer paradise where networks
of trains and buses and cabs shuffle you
around in close and sweaty anonymity

A Pokerwork of Poems

We really are barbarians with no idea of
what really matters so best you avoid any
possible clash of outlooks that may leave
you shaking your educated heads at us

Stay where you are
Don't leave your comfortable cities
You are so right
It's hell out here !

John S. Langley

In the Final Analysis

What history do we take with us
What history do we leave
and how much of it was true

What words do we take with us
What words do we leave
and which of them were true

What lives do we live in life
Who's lives do we touch upon
and were our intentions true

What, which, who, how much
When do we need to ask
and where do we state our case
and why can't we just let it pass

What More

Coffee
Sunshine
and You

What more could a man ask?

A bacon butty - with the fat done crispy

A Red Ferrari - of my size

A season ticket - V.I.P

A big yacht - with a quiet engine

A round-the-world cruise - in a suite

Nothing more
Nothing that really matters

John S. Langley

By the Lakeside

There was a picture on the wall
A print of a Lake District scene
Hand tint water-coloured

Green brown Fells dominate
an expanse of blue green water
Cows drinking at the edge

And in the foreground two
people, a man and a woman, sit
their backs to the viewer

They are sitting close probably
holding hands but we cannot
be sure, cannot quite see

My Mother bought this picture
and said in an off-hand moment
that she had made a deal

with my Father that whoever died
first would wait for the other
beside that very lakeside

I remember saying that this was
not a greatly positive thing to
have been talking about

but she gently disagreed saying
it was a comfort to them both
I should remember that

John S. Langley

***

When my mother followed my
father and left us alone
I did not remember

It was when we were clearing
the house, no longer home
that I saw it again

I looked with watering eyes
looked again and saw the
two figures backs

And was sure, sure as I could
be that my Mother was right
and that the two figures

whose faces I could not see
were sitting close together
and holding hands

They were definitely holding hands

John S. Langley

Unknown

Worry
Overtaken
Head over heals
Into a tangle together
Their years joined at the hip
A series of inconsequential events
Unknown
The warrior's grave was dug deep
As were his deeds, but was
now overgrown green
Beneath our feet
Unknowing
Under

Spider Man

Itsy bitsy
Teeny weeny
Eight legged
Arachnid

Fanged
Multi eyed
Web spinning
Monster

Scuttles across the carpet towards my feet
Hangs from the ceiling wanting to fall
and entangle itself in my hair
Takes over the bathroom

Impatiently waiting for my wife to return
from her shopping expedition
For an upturned glass to bring an end
to my torment

John S. Langley

Melting

Ice, snow, butter, iron to liquid
Cough drops on the tongue
Fortunes frittered frivolously
over time

By fire subjected to pass or fade
gradually wreaking permanent change
as cheese upon a sandwich hot to
the tongue

As night becomes day or day to night
Hearts through pity, sympathy or love
Or overwhelmed by dismay
and sorrow

On Wings

The air pulls through feathers lifting
lifting
lifting
above the hard ground
into soft air
full of dangers

The years pull through veins pulsing
pulsing
pulsing
surviving harder times
into clearer air
full of dangers

...... and imagination

John S. Langley

The Garage

Our Dad had lots of talents
but not for D.I.Y
Though effort was expended
success just passed him by

Like when he planted a fence post
All looked good to me
But imagine our consternation
When it grew to a 12ft tree

He'd always wanted a Garage
To house his pride and joy
Built to last forever
That no elements could destroy

He measured and he measured
Till he felt he knew the score
Then asked if we could help him
So he could measure some more

He planned and mapped and totalled
Filled books with illegible scrawls
To calculate how much how many
it would take to build the walls

***

A Pokerwork of Poems

He had been born in Scotland
so was always smooching about
for things that others thought rubbish
that he couldn't do without

And so he found his materials
A stack of unwanted doors
Assorted corrugated sheeting
But nothing to do for floors

Undaunted he pummelled the surface
With sledgehammer till it was flat
rock hard until the first rains came
'It'll have to do' after that

The walls were doors nailed together
Three sides of a rectangle true
Screwed braced and also half buried
and in places cemented with glue

The roof was made up of pieces
that were never intended to meet
But coerced into place with a hammer
the structure was nearly complete

The fourth side was left very open
No doors or hinges were fitted
The awkward need to open and close
were tech limits freely admitted

***

John S. Langley

Eventually the great day was dawning
Our Dad puffed his chest out in pride
The garage stood vacant and waiting
and our little black car went inside

We couldn't control our emotions
and spontaneously started to shout
We clapped and we laughed all together
And waited for Dad to come out

We waited and waited and waited
wondering if all was still well
when out of the depths of the garage
we heard a heart-rending yell

The curses and swearing were awful
completely the air was turned blue
Our Mum put her hands to her ears
and we had to do the same too

We couldn't think what could have happened
but we knew that something was wrong
when the little car revved it's engine
and came backwards into the Sun

Slowly the driver's door opened
a seething red face did appear
'I couldn't get the bloody door open'
were all the fine words we could hear

A Pokerwork of Poems

The design of the Garage was perfect
a fit for our car there's no doubt
only a single detail omitted
no space to let you get out

Our Mother motioned for silence
as a smouldering shape did us pass
and only after the back door crashed
were we permitted to laugh

John S. Langley

***

Cautioned never to mention
the elephant sat in the room
glowering from one of the corners
filling the house with gloom

Unbowed in the days that did follow
Dad found to his evident glee
that by crawling out onto the bonnet
he could squirm past the roof and be free

And thus did the Garage full function
For many a year and a day
And Dad became extra proficient
at contortions whilst hidden away

A Pokerwork of Poems

***

When time came to leave it behind us
we had not the heart to take down
this extended part of the family
so left it 'as is' and left town

I don't know if others that followed
appreciated what we had done
we hope that they really enjoyed it
tho we never checked after we'd gone

I remember that Garage quite fondly
with its unique collection of doors
always leaking from different places
and nought but clods for the floors

But mostly I'll always remember
the tremendous amount of exertion
one man's journey to self-satisfaction
never thinking of throwing the towel in

John S. Langley

***

The lessons learnt are plain to see
if you really want to succeed
above all else the story tells
these are the things you need ...

A Dream that builds a Desire that
nothing's allowed to derail
So you can best the worst of impossible things
in the hunt for the holy grail

Until at last the day is won
(as it surely must be)

Until at last you can bask in the Sun
(providing that the Sun is out)

and simply say to all that want to hear

Look, look here

I did it

I .....
       did....
              ....it

So you see beyond mere capability

it is surely determination,

perseverance

and a tenacity of spirit

that really counts

John S. Langley

Are we there yet

Speeding our way to the hospital
with broken waters
Are we there yet?
ARE WE THERE YET!!

On the drive to the holiday Let kids
squirming in the back
Are we there yet?
Are we there yet?

Dropping off a son at University total
belongings in the boot
Are we there yet?
ARE WE THERE YET!!

Planning a Cruise in the Pacific Ocean
paying through gritted teeth
Are we there yet
Not there yet

Thank Goodness
Thank God
We're not there yet
WE'RE NOT THERE YET !!

John S. Langley

Sally

Tied to the chair grounded
by a plaster cast
Scratching dry skin flakes
with a 12" ruler

Six weeks of a double break
knitting back slowly
in the restricted dark feeling
fed up alone and down

A wet nose nudges in now
lifting fingers up
Big eyes looking concerned
paws climbing onto my lap

Tongue licking away tears
bringing laughter in
place of sadness washing away
the cold bringing hope

Sally a black and white mongrel
dog my friend my pal
instinctively knowing my need
for a caring touch

was the only one to give it
unconditionally
Her shaggy unkempt coat as soft
as her wise heart

Thank you Sally, my true true friend
I have not forgotten
50 years on and still today
I see the concern
in your eyes
and feel the softness
of your heart

John S. Langley

All the Right Moves

Rolling
 Crawling
   Standing
     Dancing
       Walking
         Running
       Walking
     Limping
   Crawling
 Dancing
   ....Dancing
           ....Dancing

No Title

For people with short attention spans
poems are brilliant
>
>
>
>
>
>
>
>
>
>
>
>
>
>
>
>
>
>
>
>
>
>

John S. Langley

.... aren't they

Deleting

A button pressed, a screen beeps
A history consigned into Trash

A disc wiped clean of messages
memories of a body turned into ash

Electrons realign uncomplaining
following strict pathways of obedience

Superimposing a new set of fleeting
synapses of an alternative existence

If only it was so easy
to forget
to forgive
to selectively remove

But it's not

John S. Langley

It's life; but not as we know it

The duvet humpbacked creature
cocooned in a child's bedroom
squirms a groaning acknowledgement
as the Sun forces slitted spears of light
across the unwelcoming space

The demon voice of the demagogue
shrills in sensitive ears as slowly,
imperceptibly she makes her plans
against him and a wary eye peers forth
through the undergrowth

of hair, matted and unkempt, greasy
with unwashed rebellion an uneasy
snake-slithering from bed to floor
to hastily locked bathroom door
emitting splashing sounds

A clock, mechanical work of bureaucratic pedagogues, clicks a remonstrating progress unsullied by the time-tick of other beings of flesh, of blood, battling internal hormonal tsunamis

And so another day begins

It's life; but not as we know it

John S. Langley

Strangers

You look quite like me
But I can't understand a word
you say

You move quite like me
But I don't get your gesture's
meaning

I smile, you smile too
But I don't know if we're smiling
at the same thing

How long have we been married ?

Getting away

Distance
Change
Holidaying
Meeting new people
Going for therapy
Avoiding the subject
Biting your tongue
Becoming a hermit on a desert island

Are all great ways
Of standing
still

John S. Langley

Magic

Take a card
Any card
Tell me what it is

Is that your card ?

See

I can do magic

I'm just not
very good
at it

Not Cricket

LBW
Bowled
Caught
Run out
Stumped
Hit Wicket
Obstruction
Double Hit

You've given me out without referral

Which did I do wrong ?

John S. Langley

The Tyne Millennium Bridge

The Tyne Millennium Bridge was opened
for our cruise with people standing
waiting to get across and waving
as we passed beneath
the winking eye
proud as Punch

But having chugged past our cruise turned
looped back around and back under
And we hid our faces from those
waiting who waved again
less heartily and with
less fingers

The buzz that you get

They drove me in a car
they did not build
Along a road
they did not lay
to their piece of heaven

We get feed-in tariffs
from the solar cells
Use the meagre benefits
we receive frugally
and seldom go down the pub

We barter fish for bread
Manure for potatoes
And the money we'll get from
the article you're writing
will certainly be put to good use

But the main thing they said
in the united stereo of
commitment to the cause
Is the buzz that we get
from being totally self-sufficient

John S. Langley

Not for the first time

He's put his foot in it again
Opened his mouth
Before thinking
Not for the first time

He wants me to explain
On his behalf
Get him out of trouble
Not for the first time

He needs to engage brain
before speaking
I've told him all this
Not for the first time

He's promised to refrain
from doing this
predictably too often
Not for the first time

And my betting is
Not for the last time either

Wobbling

I used to be able
to keep several things going
at the same time

Plate-spinning was
a speciality of mine but now
only three plates

Would not say up
for very long and even one
would wobble wildly

On its pole

Now remind me again
What was this poem supposed
To be about

Patience

I wish I had the patience of a gecko
Motionlessly waiting for lunch
to arrive
within striking distance

Or a spider sitting in a corner of its
spun web waiting for the
telltale twang
of a successful capture

Or a cat crouched in the grass with
gaze fixed on a small hole
in the ground
twitching its whiskers

Or a kestrel hovering in static motion
waiting for the grass to move
against the wind
Rock steadily focussed

Patience is a virtue I do not possess
But I envy those that do

Flying

Take my hand as
my feet leave the confines
of gravity

Let's take on the
the theory of relativity
and fly

At constant velocity
through molecules and past
quarks

I don't know the way
but we can make it up as we
go along

John S. Langley

Lunch Break

A South African Management course
And on day 4 of 10 the lunch as usual
was taken outside
in the warm sunshine
overlooking the beach
Against which the waves broke
in long powerful white-topped lines

A shout alerted us to a school of dolphins
of between 10 and 20 strong close inshore
out in front of us
Surfing the waves
with consummate ease
Leaping from the water twisting and
turning as they hit the surface splashing

The Tutor called us to return to our studies
but we stayed transfixed for 5 to 10 minutes
in uplifting communion
Their sheer joy of being
shared for these moments
before they turned and disappeared
out of our sight delighting in their element

A Pokerwork of Poems

We returned reluctantly to the air-conditioned
interior the 15 of us privileged to have grasped
a few natural moments
A reminder of importance
in a deep indecipherable way
each with their own take on what they'd seen
There are worse things than being a dolphin

John S. Langley

Travelling

If you can only walk
your world is a small place full
of gossip and intrigue and tiffs
The World is too big to imagine
full of mystery, misgivings and myths

If you have a horse
your world is a growing community
with markets and days that are holy
The World now has vague boundaries
in which old news travels too slowly

If you can sail a ship
your world is getting much bigger
and nations compete to explore
the World revealing strange places
never visited or envied before

If you can drive a car
you are independently mobile
Your neighbourhood is more
The World is shrinking towards you
It is everyone's time to explore

A Pokerwork of Poems

If you can take a plane
you are living science fiction
of less than a century ago
The World can be reached in a day
wherever you pay to go

When we can routinely go into space
and look back on our blue planet
with its extent and mysteries exposed

will we seek new worlds with old
lessons learnt

or export our imperfections
more widely

John S. Langley

The Problem is

The problem with a good death
is the effect it has on others

Leaving in the middle of a dance
is not great for the party vibe

Making off at Christmas tends to
put a dampener on the festivities

Collapsing as you're playing footie
ruins the meaning of the result

It seems you just can't have it both ways

What's good for the goose just
cocks up the plans of the gander

Three Wishes

You don't have to do everything
in just one day

Take it easy there's still time to
smell the cheese

Before tasting, savour the moment
time is your friend

So saying the genie returned
to the bottle

And the madness restarted again

John S. Langley

Sorry

Just slip that camel through
the eye of that needle
could you
for me

Just teach that pig to fly
in circles preferably
would you
for me

Just teach that silly old dog
some new magic tricks
can you
for me

Just stop the tide in its tracks
and turn it back
will you
for me

The camel squeezed through
The pig looped the loop
The dog disappeared
The tide turned

Is this enough to prove
that I really did mean it
when I said
I'm Sorry

Is it enough

What else do you want me to do

John S. Langley

Elephant

There are not many satisfactory rhymes for Elephant

Surely the solution is to be creative

Not to eliminate the Elephant

All this way

Travelled all this way and
all you want is a burger

You say it's not like home
where the streets are clean
and water's drunk from the tap

If you want all of that
stay home

But I just nod and say
'Everywhere's different'

John S. Langley

Between There and Here

It looked so far when viewed
from There
But now I'm Here and look
back
over my shoulder
it looks so near that I could
touch it

It was Where I couldn't wait
to be
A far point to aim towards
Then
But now I'm Here
I wonder what all the fuss
was about

A Pokerwork of Poems

***

The journey has been mainly
fun
Though the track has not been
straight
And I would run
it over again but at a different
rate

John S. Langley

Advertising

For the mature man
Means: You need to have money

Clothes for every woman
Means: We've got really big sizes too

In need of modernisation
Means: This would be a mega project

Great value for money
Means: Don't expect these goods to last

I have a little money
Come in oversize XL
Am in need of renovation
But either way this offer
ain't gonna last forever

The Look

How do you do it

The look was almost imperceptible
But it pierced me like a thunderbolt
                            cutting
                   through
            me
      to
   the
core

Sending a shiver
through my soul

How do you do that

John S. Langley

What Cannot Be Erased

I've been here
We met
Three offspring resulted
Adding to
the human race

My DNA is
sprinkled
in all kinds of places
adding to
the Earth's crust

My breath has
conjoined
with the atmosphere
adding to
Global warming

We will leave
our mark
but I'm not sure if
we leave it
a better place

John S. Langley

Zonal Differences

Jet lagged in Hanoi
I can't recall my own name
I don't know if I'm floating or drowning
Both sensations feel the same

My mind cannot grasp
The concept of flying for 12 hours
for a 6 hour time difference

The disconnect is not apparent
in my current state of mind and
swirls around
without solution
making me giddy

In the wee small disquieting hours of
the morning
early evening
I receive your text

glowing torch bright beside my bed

and reach
and read
with unfocused eyes

without understanding

re-read
re-read
mechanically
without process, comprehension,
assimilation

And fall back on the pillow
exhausted
hoping to slip back into
the unstable blackness

Hoping the world will stop turning
giving my mind time to rebalance

John S. Langley

Playful Sleep

When sleep doesn't come
refuses doggedly to cooperate
It doesn't help to
count sheep
get a drink
splash you face in cold water

When sleep decides not to cooperate
turns its back on your pleading
It doesn't matter if you
stretch your legs
switch on the radio
take a herbal remedy

When sleep connives to play
these tricks only one thing
is for sure
you will
fall fast asleep
at last

10 minutes before
the alarm goes off

Good Intentions

The sign over the door said

Discovery Room

And then in bigger
graphic text
Curved to match
the arc of the doorway

Keep Creating ; Keep Dreaming

So
intrigued
I went to have a look

But the door was locked
And the lights were off

John S. Langley

1000 years

Does 1000 years of conflict
make forgiveness somehow easier
because peace is such a precious thing
that even atrocities can be assimilated
without revenge
to try to make it
last

If we hurt each other just once
why is forgiveness so difficult
if peace is such a precious thing to us
or can a single hurt not be assimilated
as we both wait
for what might happen
next

Stuck in the Groove

The girl I kissed
The things I missed
Acting like a clown
The reason I left town

The girl I missed
The things I kissed
Grinning like a clown
On the day that I left town

The jar, the jar I moved
that jarred the needle
out of the groove

And now I'm stuck like a broken record
playing the same part
of the same tune
over and over and over

and

over, over, over, over, over ....

until the record wears out

John S. Langley

Something to wake up to

Good morning and welcome to the show

This morning, like every morning,
we'll be talking to some ladies and gents
who believe they're important

and have something crucial to say
and who were able to get up
at this ungodly hour
of the morning

We, your proxy, and proud to be so,
will ask, on your behalf,
the most ludicrous,
inconsequential questions

that are on the outer margins
of possibility and then we'll interrupt
repeatedly to ensure we're unable
to get a proper answer

Then we'll discuss the inadequacies
real or imagined or both
between ourselves
because we know

how fond of our dulcet tones
you all are
at this time of a morning

John S. Langley

***

We'll also make time for sport,
as we recognise that not all our
listeners are public school bred

and we want to accommodate
well, let's just say, the less intellectual
factions among you

We'll break the News of the latest list
of disastrous defeats
as sensitively as we can,
without really caring,
or understanding the rules

A Pokerwork of Poems

And then there's the weather,
there's always the weather,
and just in case you're hard of hearing
we'll repeat our reports of
yesterday's weather every 5 minutes
or so and bamboozle you
with varying forecasts for the day ahead,
giving you so many choices that whatever
actually occurs we cannot possibly
be accused of getting it wrong.

John S. Langley

We'll avoid defaulting to the obvious
although you may detect it in our tone,
that the weather reflects our country as
'It'll normally be crap anywhere North of
Watford (it's all they deserve) whereas
sunglasses and shorts are the order of the
day here in the more cultured South.'

Oh yes, and
please don't let me forget
we also have the beeps,

Beep
        Beep
                Beeeeeeeeep

You

You lose my rhythm
You refuse to rhyme
You give me palpitations

You're stubborn as a mule
You're strong-willed to a fault
You ruin my meditations

You'll drive me crazy
You'll push me over the top
You pro my crastinations

You, You, You, You

The You I can't forget

You're the one I can't forget

You'll never be forgotten

John S. Langley

Golden Book

I'll write my life in a book of Gold
carve unique characters into the
yellow metal
that will not tarnish
with the years

Will the memory of my life be as precious
as the cold Gold on which it is carefully
inscribed
that will not tarnish
with the years

Or will my life be melted down and lost
in the heartless heat, the yellow flow of
molten metal
that will not tarnish
with the years

I will bury my Golden Book deep down
in the unknowing ground, away from
grasping hands
so its worthlessness
will not tarnish
with the years

John S. Langley

Bartering

I needed a hat
and asked the price
250

Too much, too much
said a stranger to my right
You've got to haggle, he said
I can see you're not a seasoned traveller
100

The old lady whistled
and shook her head and
reached for another hat
This 100

It's the quality she said,
you can feel the difference
Here feel
I felt I would like the better hat
I said

Good choice, he said,
it's a nice hat
but now you've shown her
you're interested
she's got you

150, I said
OK,
OK she said
grimacing
but too quickly

The man tutted and
clicked his tongue
I like the hat, he said,
let me show you how
it's done

Another, like that, he said
No more, she said
Last one, she said
I really like that hat, he said
No more, sorry, sorry

He looked glum

You want to buy a hat, I said
250

John S. Langley

What is Knowledge

Knowledge is the light

Clean water to bathe and drink
Providing enough food to eat
Medicines to restore health
Transportation to travel far and wide
Power for light and so many
other things

Knowledge is the darkness
That protects our light

How to poison
How to misuse drugs for money
Jet Fighters, Helicopters, Drones
The bomb

A Pokerwork of Poems

Knowledge is the light
That leads us into darkness

John S. Langley

View from Aesop's Bridge

I'm like the dog
Who looked over the edge
of the bridge's parapet
and dropped his bone
into the river
hoping for a bigger one

I'm like the bone
Hitting the water with a splash
Being taken by the current
turning over and over
end on end
A leg bone
running away

I'm like the water
filling the river with
strong currents beneath
a deceitfully static
glassily polished surface

Or gurgling and spitting
against rocks and stones
wearing them smooth
with time

Looking back up at the dog
Giggling

John S. Langley

Lotus

Centuries patiently pass
a pod
buried deep in the cracked
and dry earth

Until life-giving waters
flood in
and chase growth upwards breaking
the surface

and there burst forth a bloom
white, red
encouraging the journey
to 10,000 good deeds
in this life

3:

Growing Embers

Moving in the 4th Dimension

We can move forward or back (+x , -x)
We can move left or right (+y, -y)
We can move up or down (+z, -z)
So why, if time is the 4th dimension,
can we only go one-way (+t, ??)

I get the bit that messing with your own
timeline sets up an insoluble paradox
but,

why can't we make an appointment
to meet last Tuesday

or eat breakfast in 3 different continents
on the same day
at the same time

Think of the mess we would make of the
World's monetary systems

That alone makes it worth considering

John S. Langley

Cavernous

Peering into a dark deep enough
for riddles
Water sculpted masses
shift their shape in differing shades
to bring safe harbour to some
fear to others

Perhaps here flames flickered often
on feasting
Or animals resided
licking their wounds clean as bats
danced towards the moonlight
hunting in packs

A Pokerwork of Poems

An illusory permanence fills the place
as water
drips change through
every fissure and crack
dissolves the present
buries the past
to build a new layer

John S. Langley

Sacred Object

Valuable only by
association

Sitting in plain view
A Shell
Curled protective
Residence
Empty
Deserted

A Pokerwork of Poems

Object of importance
But no value
Joining together
Events remembered
Carefully lifted
To hear that Sea again

John S. Langley

First Meal

19 hours you kept us waiting
in the Maternity ward
pain and exhaustion mingled
with anxiety about why and what
was happening

When you finally deigned to arrive
to leave your warm
liquid embracing cocoon you
made a mess on the floor that I had
to paddle through

letting go of a hand now relaxing
while your fingers
and toes were counted, your
airways cleared and lungs successfully
tested for volume

to find a seat in a corner and unwrap
silver foiled food
revealing previous day's cheese
and tomato in white bread wet with time
but appetising

to someone who has not eaten
Taking a bite
to the midwife's surprise who
thought at least I could have left the
birthing room first

But this was my first meal as a Dad
Why would I want to be
anywhere else

John S. Langley

Group Tour

Travelers thrown together by the
economics of group travel
Getting along for the common good
and mutual benefit in foreign lands
Strangers

Abdicating leadership to their guide
as path of least resistance
No competition for the Alpha male
position as the tour is short enough
Collusion

Journeying in companionable truce
for a fragment of shared time
Parting foreseen at a distance of days
as relationships strengthen or break
Manoeuvring

A Pokerwork of Poems

Paths parted at airport lounge doors
to return to absentee living
Mementos and memories conjoin in
exaggerated tellings to unlistening ears
Returning

Starting already to mentally plan
the next go on the
Carousel

John S. Langley

Beaumont Hamel

There are ghosts behind the stones
Looking at us from
lost eyes
Unable to weep over
lost lives

A long way to come to fall
so quickly into the
liquid earth
Open to the closing of
their day

Lives are in the mist that drifts
past the hundred-year
-later heads
taking digital images
of stones

A Pokerwork of Poems

Paying homage to what they
cannot comprehend
not seeing
the lines of ghosts looking on
looking out

John S. Langley

Smile

Whose smile is that
lying on the floor
in a pool of teardrops

Is there present
in that mouth the
tender cheeky cheerfulness

Be careful not to
step on that smile
if it breaks
it may leave
no trace

Nonsense

Isn't it better
to get wetter
than a hippopotamus

Isn't it sweeter
to be neater
than a cat's licked whisker

Can a rhino
lay my lino
in the upstairs bathroom

If I'm not here again today
remind me that I've gone away
but if your entreaties I ignore
please don't bother me any more

I've obviously gone for help

John S. Langley

Final Frontier

Traveling at the speed of light
for 20,000 years
in suspended animation

Making first contact with alien
life forms with arms
and legs waving in semaphore

The only common word in our
vocabulary seems to be
'Starbucks'
even here
at the final frontier

Can it be that they got here first

It must be a tax haven

World Heritage Site :

A site of World importance

To be protected for future generations

By being trampled underfoot
on new concrete footpaths
as crowds of well-meaning tourists
spend their money

A success story

A means by which we can ensure
we ruin things a little bit
more slowly, slowly, slowly
and by committee

John S. Langley

Between Enemy Lines

Have you had a good day
What have you been doing
Are you hungry
Where have you been

It's been no different to any day
You know the job stinks, salary's crap
I'm starving hungry
And in hope of something edible

Ethel came round today
I want to leave
Said they're all doing well
I've had enough of this

Oh did she, very good
Spitting poison I guess
I'm pleased they're doing so well
I can't go on like this

There's something we should talk about
There's something we should talk about

But not right now

Enemies

At the distance of propaganda
warring principles impersonalised
and warriors demonised into
right versus wrong

Sinews strengthen to purpose
and unleash vigour amongst youth
watching each other's backs
in line of fear

Imperative not to meet any
enemy face to face in calm water
that may risk recognition of
mutual humanity

John S. Langley

Sculpted

Inside seasoned wood
a hundred year awakening
is formulated

Marble veined red
black, yellow block awaits
the chisel strike

Water frozen to rock
sees its own future inside
shaped to clarity

Half emerged the face
is roughly grained contours
seeking identity

A Pokerwork of Poems

Reaching a completion
not final, a next phase only
deserving attention

Impassive representation
of another's creative insight
stares in silence

Into an unknown future

John S. Langley

Who Knows

It was difficult as you
ranted and raved
and spun like a top
on the kitchen floor
to see the type of man
you might become

As you grew in strength
of mind as well as
body your stubborn
streak stood exposed
to the elements and
turbulence of mood

In teenage times you
learnt about friendship
and the effect on others
of peer pressure and
the responsibilities that
come with actions

A Pokerwork of Poems

Who could have seen
the man within the child
that you have become
The man within that child
that makes us proud
to have known you

Who can ever see

John S. Langley

Sorry

I'm sorry but to carry on
I had to avoid thinking
Make no time out of the little time
available

So selfish a way to handle
something that bit so
deeply into all our lives needing to
carry on

Even now when looking back
I know there would
have been no better way for me
to cope

But I'm sorry so sorry that
I couldn't be more
of a support when I know you
needed it

And I never said the sorry
I meant to say when
able to start removing the
armour plating

A Pokerwork of Poems

I say it now - I'm sorry
You knew me well
so I hope you knew already
and it's not
too late

too late to say sorry

John S. Langley

Reflexology

Electric shocks flick the tension
from my body through
my fingers
pulled by yours

The cedar smell of the oils you use
fills my weary senses
with peaceful
notes of therapy

Even though you're my Mother
I'm pleased you did
this course
and only wonder

When can you do this again

Butterfly

Outside the window in November
unseasonably bright with colour
delicate wings veined in black
you patter at the glass

Drawing attention from our inside
chatter of times past memories
of you with smiling through teacups
and cakes with cream

I wish you were here I wish you were
as the big wings carry you up
Away into clear cold blue after popping by
to say your goodbyes

John S. Langley

Get a hat

Bought a straw hat
a panama in style
pale in complexion
from a street vendor
just right to shade
my eyes from the Sun

If you want to get ahead
get a hat

Unpredicted rain fell
to wet from top to
soaking brim that dipped
to drip upon my nose
cold droplets from a grey
rebuking sky

If you want to get ahead
get a hat

The colour darkened
as it drooped around
my brow the hatband
sweating leaking dye

in a circular henna ring
without my knowing

If you want to get ahead
get a hat

Alerted by grinning
reflection confirmed
the new look acquired
The person I procured it
from had sensibly moved on
so I was left to contemplate

at my own leisure
hoping the stain would
disappear with time
and in the meantime
I would need another hat
to hide my embarrassment

from a shop this time
once bitten twice shy

If you want to get ahead
get a (good quality) hat

John S. Langley

The News

When I came into the room
you had gone
Sitting there on the sofa
the News on
The cat bringing me in to
find you

I told you not to leave me
but you waited
until I wasn't looking without
saying goodbye
After a good day we'd spent
together

Just as you wished it to be
The News on
a cup of tea by your hand
that I hold
as it grows colder and I
contemplate

A Pokerwork of Poems

all the years that went so
fast past us
the ups, the downs, the ups
the laughter
your laugh and I wonder how
I tell the kids

John S. Langley

Playing

Peering from the woodshed
or a Pirate's camp

Spying on a crocodile
or a lump of wood

Fighting off the Dinosaurs
or chasing next door's cat

Flying to the Moon and back
or running round the corner

Which of these I really did
I really can't remember

All that really matters now
is that I did them - twice

Give 'em

Give 'em boots to grow into
and things to try
Give 'em books to grow into
and to ask why

Give 'em things to grow out of
and eggs to fry
Give 'em books to grow out of
and hope they'll try

Give 'em permission to go
and the wings to try
Give 'em roots to grow
and wings to fly

Give 'em roots to grow
and wings to fly

John S. Langley

Short but Sweet

I knew
I was in
a foreign country
when the taxi driver
said

I had
given him
too much money

and gave me some of it
back

Full Moon

Full Moon glitters on
lanterns drifting
down a river

Each flame a symbol
of hopes wished
for someone

Or in thanks for help
already received
by lucky ones

For practical things
money and luck
and success

For one month only
till Full again the
Moon offers

another chance

John S. Langley

One Bus

They came from England
Ireland
Scotland, Wales
Spain......

Farmer, teacher, accountant
Builder
Engineer, electrician
Retired .....

One bus, one free day spent
Shopping
Walking, cooking class
Spa, beach......

Each to their own

One bus
One trip
Different journeys

Communicating

Talking, nodding, winking
Emails, texts, messaging
Facebook, You Tube
My Space
Skype

We are compulsive communicators

Except for boys
They're mainly crap at it

John S. Langley

Tourist Invasion

Welcome shopping soldiers
with pockets full of gold
Don't believe the horror stories
we know that you've been told

We're really very friendly
There'll be no kind of fuss
Any problems you might come across
you can leave with us

And as long as you have dollars
you'll be greeted with a smile
and to get those dollars from you
we'll go that extra mile

A Pokerwork of Poems

But when your pockets empty
please please be on your way
For we have others coming
We hope you enjoyed your stay

John S. Langley

Winter's Heroes

Sharp was the cold and hoar the frost
that lay on the land and set the white hairs
rigid in the old man's beard

So that there was a crunch and a
crackle when he lay hand to it stroking
absently through in thought

The gnarled oaken door he approaches
shines under and around and through with yellow
light signaling fire within

Spied afar the watchman waits and
asks and goes in and returns with message
to enter and sit and eat

A Pokerwork of Poems

Passing quietly he sits and
warms as bid and eats answering soberly
the slurred queries from young men

in beer soaked brown beards clothed in bear,
antelope, and wolf and unsteady from
the long feasting and the drink,

mostly from the drink, thick, hoppy,
frothy, fresh, healthy in moderation
now far surpassed on this night

Soon the Master of the Hall calls
him to the centre close enough to the fire
to risk singeing, or frizzling

John S. Langley

his bleached white hair, of scorching
pock-marked skin, wise eyes rheumy in the glow
glittering under tangled brows

His deep worn and wrinkled skin tanned
brown and he, older still than his years, chants
loud and full of gusto songs

of battles won, lost in times past
and in times to come of real and mythic
beasts and heroes interwoven

as truth and lies interwoven
to suit the ear of the cheering, churring,
raucous men and their women

A Pokerwork of Poems

who pretend to listen but whose
heads are heaving with more important things,
real for the night practical

for the morrow while the Bard sings
to answer the calls for known and lost tales
and new ventures and new words

that hold fast the Hall until his voice
drops and in somnolent husky tone he tells
of life and death and sleep and

valour and unforgotten names,
reverent, head-healing, reassuring,
as hope-filling words bringing

John S. Langley

full meaning to all and purpose
to the future as the noise begins to
subside the fire collapses

and embers dart with yellow tongues
The tangle bearded man gratefully takes
the proffered payment in hand

tucks food away, the grease salving
grasping fingers and slips away past night
watchers nod steps out once more

into the breath fogged dark bathed silver
by the Moon and trudges deep set footprints
that will be gone by morning

A Pokerwork of Poems

Inside staying sleep overwhelms
the winter heroes dogs chew discarded
scraps of bone and tear sinew

and a few wide eyed children hide in
the shadows chewing over what they have seen
and heard, grinning to each other

John S. Langley

I'll teach you

I'll teach you
I can sulk for a week
See

I'll teach you
I can live like hermit
and suffer in silence
See

I'll teach you
I can criticise everyone
find no one I like
and no one to like me
See

I'll teach you
I told you one of these days
I'd teach you and I have
Where've you gone
Where've you gone
to now

Tigers

Living with the tiger can be
a dangerous thing
one mistake can be fatal
one misstep

A tiger can
also provide protection
Living without a tiger can be
a dangerous thing

Living can be a dangerous thing
Ask a tiger

John S. Langley

Holiday Development

This is nice let's
p-p-p-put up an hotel
with 35 Floors
and a casino

What a nice view let's
p-p-p-put down a golf course
with 3 different courses
and a spa

Let's concrete over half of it
s-s-s-so we can view the rest
without having to step outside
into the open air

We'll package up the sunshine
r-r-r-redirect the rain
so that our V.I.P's
can't get wet

A Pokerwork of Poems

We can make money here
u-u-u-until we wreck the place
then we can give it back
and go to somewhere else

Where I'm sure they'll be happy
with w-w-w-what we can do
for them

John S. Langley

The Flow of Knowledge

Winding flow full
of eddies
equations swirling
mathematics

He said, She said
alternatives
bobbing now one
now the other

Tributaries joining
now and again
from any direction
muddying waters

then settling clearing
rushing on
gathering speed around
the next bend

A Pokerwork of Poems

And the next, never
settling, never
final, growing, turning back
flowing forward

flowing through the
still unknown

John S. Langley

Power Cut

5 star luxury
plunged into blackness
by a flashing bolt
flicks a switch from
smiling sophistication
to survival of the fattest

Leech tight companions
disengage with new priorities
running for exits
that don't exist
new blindness breaking
the veneer of class

Then light comes back on
power is restored to the wealthy
who shuffle back
to their croissants
and apologising hangers-on
know their future

A Pokerwork of Poems

Cursing fate
Unfair fate
Unfair

And the lights go out again

John S. Langley

Harmony

Sky
Me
Land
Now right here
where I stand

Parents
Me
Children
Shifting seeking
equilibrium

You
Me
Chance
Accepting the norm
of turbulence

A Pokerwork of Poems

Then
Me
Then
Recalled into the
green unknown

Sky
Me
Land
Tomorrow where
will I stand

John S. Langley

Bananas

I'm not too superstitious
but when I bought a bunch of
bananas and shared them
the rain stopped and
the Sun came out

Was it the bananas, was
it the sharing or was the rain
going to stop and the Sun
come out anyway
No matter what

I went back
to buy more bananas

Lessons in Recycling

Colours dance in russet red
and yellow gold

as winds and first frosts free
leaf hold

and loose to fly in fluttering
downward glide

to earth that groans hoar white
with cold

and time leaches to slick brown
to black

to become one with wet soil
through mould

and be washed down to become
nutrients

ready for a new year and return
to green

John S. Langley

Juxtaposition

Protect our Planet
It's our home

Blazed the electric
advertising sign

Before flicking over to
the next ad

for a type of 4x4 vehicle
essential for

problem-free travel and
a happy life

……….. presumably just
a short one

Limits

Are there things poems cannot be
written about

Or it is that there are things that
a poet cannot write

I cannot write about this thing
There is no mirth in it
No light relief

No I cannot write about this

John S. Langley

Reactions

Hand, fingers, tips of fingers
intertwine like blue and yellow
making green

Two individuals clear in their
own right together make a fresh
distinct combination

Caustic and Acid with competing
properties make Salt together
essential for life

Reactions fizz, effervesce or
run together smoothly or
argue to cohabit

So it is
So it should be
So it has ever been

Fragments

…… and everything was going well until the ninth day …….

…… and then it happened…….

…… and when we got back we were never the same …….

……. well you can't be can you ……

John S. Langley

Grouchy

Why are you feeling grouchy

I'm 4 it's how I'm meant to get the
attention I deserve
(when I need it)

I'm a teenager we're programmed
to be grouchy
(with our parents)

I'm 42 leave me alone and give me
some space
(to be grouchy)

I'm old and I'm allowed to be anything
I damn well want
(within reason)

Why are you feeling grouchy

Cheer up

Trust

You had the trust
to fall asleep in my arms
knowing I would not drop you

Your eyes closed
your steady breathing chest
rising and falling in gentle rhythm

Mouth open and
closing in milky post-burp
gurgles that make us smile at you

Sleep little thing
long may your trust last
we'll do our best not to break it

John S. Langley

Completely up to you

You can go and see the scruffy
little car that is falling apart
Or the nice shiny black one with
almost no mileage that runs like
a dream

It's completely up to you
Which would you like?

We can take you to a grotty hotel
with bedbugs and fleas
Or the new modern one with clean
spacious rooms currently offering
a discount

It's completely up to you
Which would you like?

A Pokerwork of Poems

I can offer you this ticket for a show
nobody likes with limited view
Or a ticket for this show that is the
toast of the town with a clear view
of the stage

It's completely up to you
Which would you like?

We can argue about this all night
and end not speaking for hours
Or you can apologise for being an
idiot and I'll forgive you and be
nice again

It's completely up to you
Which would you like?

Outside

The ceiling is painted eggshell blue
with pointed silver stars

It blocks out the sky that above it
is dark with thunderclouds

and pours down rain that clatters and
gushes through unseen gutters

whilst inside dry under their sky
the people sing of Harvest time

Proof of Efficacy

Eyes are painted
On the prow of our boats
To ward off Dragons

The painted eyes
are also effective against
bad spirits and

Sea monsters that
would seek unseen to drag
us to the bottom

How do we know it works?

Have you seen any
Dragons
Bad Spirits or
Sea Monsters
around here lately?

John S. Langley

Oppression

Bellow ground the air is hot
and humidly sticky
Rivulets of your own juice
congeal and flow

over skin oppressed by the
weight of earth
Above is earth, below is earth and
earth pushes your insides

constricting your breathing as
through gritted teeth
irregular eyes search
in the darkness

for a glimmer of natural light
that might crack the black for
fingers to scrabble towards
and try to break through

A Pokerwork of Poems

Arms then stretching upwards
feeling for cool air
Seeking the extra strength
to last

to last another day

John S. Langley

Vultures

The vulture climbing high
circles and sees
for miles

Watches the puffs of smoke
the sharp retort
of killing

Stoically looks on as the food
is prepared to be
eaten hot

Waits for quiet to descend
on thermal wings
to feasting

And even though there is
far too too much
for everyone

A Pokerwork of Poems

Squabbles with others over
the pecking order
then gorges

Amidst the stooping bodies
ferreting out shiny
inedible things

Today is a good day
to be a vulture

There are lots of days
like this

John S. Langley

Through your eyes

Through your eyes
I see others

Your uniqueness templated
through chance

Absorbing the new world avidly
like a sponge

Colours
Hard Soft
Smooth Rough
Hot Cold

Good Bad
Bad Good

My Child

Don't learn too fast
Don't look too deeply

Retain a child's eye
for as long as you can

John S. Langley

Battle of the Sexes

When it comes to the
little things
women rule

Like giving Birth
Breast feeding
Deciding what to eat and when

Keeping clean
Choosing the right
colours for the bathroom

Not liking war
Talking more
Drinking less

But men
make all the
big decisions

Like strategy
Reading a map
Determining a position
on significant Global Issues

Men know
when they have made
the right choice
from the look
on their wife's face

John S. Langley

Kingfisher

Flashing incandescent blue
One with the river

Over boats repaired over repairs
Peeling paint caulked watertight

Over people's lives intertwined
One with the river

Patiently waiting and watching
for the right moment to dive

Incandescent flashing blue
One with the river

Awakenings

Leaves rustle like water
in a stream of wind

Water like brown milk
carries sustenance

Wind and rain embrace
in a whirlpool dance

And the world turns on
a silver penny piece

Whilst inside the room
all is expectation

As life begins and ends
on the toss of a coin

John S. Langley

Proving Memory is not Random

If 1% of what you do is remembered
(and that's a lot)

If 5% of what we do is worth remembering
(and that would be a lot)

Then there is only a 1 in 2,000 chance
of remembering anything of significance

But I remember every wrong word
I ever said to you

every instance
every moment
every thought

every finely honed pointed barb
every intentional hurt
every sulking defamation

So memory
My memory
All memory
is clearly not random

Q.E.D

John S. Langley

The Magician

Look
In my hand
You can see the ball

Now
Look again
It's gone - like Magic

Look
In my heart
You can see your pain

Now
Look again
It's there - like Magic

Look
In your heart
Look out for your pain

Smile
Look again
It's gone - like Magic

John S. Langley

Three Little Words

In the first flush mentioned
as often as breathing
those three little words

And later less but more felt
and lightly appreciated
those three little words

With time more occasional
as fallen from grace
those three little words

So rare and avoided as time's
tether takes toll on
those three little words

And now you've just said them
they ripple right through me
with electric effect
with delight unexpected
with chest proudly heaving
with heart all a flutter
with surprise and amazement

those three little words

A Pokerwork of Poems

'You're right darling'

John S. Langley

Picking over the Ruins

Broken stone is scattered that
once were walls
high strong impregnable
now laid low by time and robbery

Clambering along in single file
looking only at feet
for a safer footing
not looking up or back but down

Other's footsteps have indented
the ancient surface
polished and worn it
to a smoothness made for slipping

The ruins make loud accusation
of too little effort
made in restoration
'Look at what happens' they cry

A Pokerwork of Poems

to deaf ears intent only on
a repeat destruction
and the feet echo back
headed in determinedly different directions

Hunting for more solid ground
amongst the shifting sands

John S. Langley

Age

When the big white hunter
becomes a champion of conservation
and weeps in the night

Or when the shopaholic starts
to visit charity shops in daylight and
actively recycles rubbish

Or when the rich man begins
to give money away because of a
failing belief in immortality

Or when the father puts the
future earnings of his children and
grandchildren above his own

Age cannot be inherited
we must make the same mistakes
over and over

and again

Perhaps until time runs out
for mistakes

John S. Langley

The Photograph

Smiling for the camera
between bickering fights
the camera tells
a thousand lies

The album pages turned
corners evidence of frequent
revisiting of what
might have been

Time and tide depleting
the number of knowing eyes
that see through
behind the image

As into history passes
an unchallenged falsehood
a frozen slice
of inaccuracy

Use of Language

Misunderstand me in Italian
Throw me a curveball in Spanish
Dance a verbal jig in Swahili
Utter a sage phrase in Mandarin

Evaluate my chances in Swedish
Write me a limerick in German
Impress my friends in Arabic
Lead me astray in provincial French

So many choices to miscommunicate

Which one will you choose today

To keep me on my toes

John S. Langley

Names Matter

No,
you can't call me
by my given name
that can be changed by deed poll
There are three of you
that've got no choice
You have to call me Dad

I know that you
are all grown up
into big strong men it's true
but that doesn't mean
I've changed as much
You have to call me Dad

It may not be
the modern way
and almost obsolete
but it's my name
and I'm sticking to it
You have to call me Dad

A Pokerwork of Poems

Your partners and
your girlfriends can
call me what they like
but unfortunately it's
not the same for you
You have to call me Dad

You see the thing
is this my boys
I'm proud of each of you
and whatever may
happen along the way
I'll always be your Dad

So,
You have to call me Dad

You need to call me Dad

John S. Langley

Owl Box

We bought an 'Owl Box'
and risking life and limb
hauled it up a tree to secure it
at the recommended height
for 'Owl Boxes'

It had a big white sign
with clear black letters
'Owl Box' to avoid any doubt
about the one intended purpose
for an 'Owl Box'

The first year there were
Jackdaws and an awful
lot of noise with young looking
like terra-dactyls who couldn't read
the sign 'Owl Box'

The second year brought
Wood Pigeons coo-cooing
instead of the woo-woo-wooing
that was called for by the designated
sign 'Owl Box'

A Pokerwork of Poems

The third year the box
looked empty and starting
to fall away from the tree
although you could still clearly read
the sign 'Owl Box'

And then one sunny day
a small fluffy face appeared
A female Tawny Owl was nesting
and three owlings were the result in
the 'Owl Box'

Proving beyond doubt that
perseverance through
incompetence
sometimes does
pay off

And Owls can read

John S. Langley

Branching Out

Their mother's calling cries
fluffy chicks out of their element
into daylight

To claw with big eyes unsteadily
along branches clustering together
for protection

As feathers form and sleekness
flaps virgin wings to repeated stretches
and to test

Waiting their mother fed moment
who entices cajoles entreats first flight
a leap of faith

And flap and lift and grasp and gain
confident strength against gravity's
push and pull

A Pokerwork of Poems

Away and up and glide and longer
and further distance as it reaches

their time ....
                    to branch out

John S. Langley

Maps

Engineering
Science
Art
Meet on a single page
in high definition

Paper making
Printing
Colouring
Point the way anywhere
using a compass

History
Culture
Language
Flavour the hidden meanings
wrapped in time

And we still lose our way
arguing over the dulcet tones
of the female SatNav voice
calmly turning us off the road
into a field

to get us stuck

If you want to get to there
I wouldn't start from here

John S. Langley

En Route

Fly me to Barbados
It's so wonderfully sounding
Bar
       ba
             dos

Take me to see an Orangutan
Redheads with their wise eyes
 O
    rang
        ut
            an

Lead me into temptation
Before it's too late to appreciate it
temp
        ta
           tion

We can leave this room of antiseptic
and go anywhere we can imagine
an
    ti
       sep
          tic

Hold my hand ready for embarkation
here we go here we go to anywhere
we're ready for
Em
    bar
       kat
          ion

Don't you dare leave without me

John S. Langley

Ghosts

Floorboards creaking in the dead
of night

Step by step bringing the fear of fear
ever closer

Approaching the shut bedroom door
not locked

As we lie under covers close wrapped
eyes wide

The fickle brass doorknob winks at the
silver moonlight

And we watch we watch and we see it
start to move

to turn in the night as we listen in to
every little sound ....

Then the door opens

www.ingramcontent.com/pod-product-compliance
Lightning Source LLC
Chambersburg PA
CBHW062052280426
43673CB00089B/489/J